Likes Don't Pay Bills

Five Social Media Marketing Myths

By: Alan Owen and Sunbird Marketing

Table of Contents

Introduction

Social media marketing has devolved into "tricking" people to click on an ad rather than to spread the word about you or your product organically. Of course, the ultimate goal is to drive users to view your products and services on your website and to continuously gain new subscribers, customers or followers. It is a process of building awareness.

Through social media, the direct connection with your customers or potential customers has now become less personal. Businesses have to simulate human contact from behind a screen in such a way as to make a person WANT to click, like and share simply by the way in which they are engaged.

In this book, we will discuss the many strategies involved and the mindset that you need to have in order to properly and effectively drive traffic to your site, products or services, not only to generate a one-time sale or even a one-time customer. The bigger picture and where your mindset needs to be is to bring awareness to the product or service and draw additional followers and ultimately, customers.

We will discuss the five biggest myths surrounding social media marketing and what you can do instead to drive traffic. This book will be full of actionable advice that will drastically change your view on marketing and more importantly, social media marketing.

Let's first begin with exactly what social media marketing is and how to use it to your benefit. Social media marketing is a strategy to manage the engagement with possible customers to transform the scope of the business and to expand the reach. By using various social media platforms, businesses are able to reach a larger base of people, targeting different groups with different campaigns and messages.

If you are completely new to the social media marketing arena, you may not be aware of some of these platforms, many of which will be discussed later: Pinterest, Facebook, LinkedIn, Twitter, and Instagram. Each platform of course has its own system as well as diverse users.

So, let's jump right in!

Part I: The Five Myths

Advertisements have always been a good way to ensure that your product or service gets the exposure that you need. In the past, all the advertising was done through physical mediums – such as flyers, newspaper ads, and a variety of other ads like that. Nowadays, however, everything is done through the Internet. Social media – and general SEO techniques – have made it quite easy for us to get our product out there and become quite known on the market.

That being said, social media and good digital advertising is a very efficient way of ensuring that your product gets the exposure that it needs. People are looking up everything online nowadays – and with that, companies have begun investing more and more into digital marketing.

The most popular method of increasing the visibility of your brand is to advertise it on Facebook. Considering that there are currently billions of people on the platform, it is one of the most efficient ways to get your product out there – all by using likes and shares. Instagram is also very efficient for getting your brand across, particularly if you are handling a business with quite a lot of visual appeal.

That being said, many business owners have their own beliefs when it comes to social media – and they swear by certain myths that are not relevant even though they make sense. These myths have been circulating for quite some time – and while they may not be true, some people believe they are. Because of that, they end up with smaller conversions and fewer clients.

These myths may vary from business owner to business owner – and depending on your approach, your business may also suffer from it. Some people believe that their followers care about them – but in truth, they care about what you can give them. This "giving" can be physical or psychical (a product vs. a funny or interesting post). However, the truth is that these people care less about you as a person – feel less concerned about you – and more about the informational value that a certain post provides them with.

There are also those people that believe that the more likes you get, the better – or that the more you post at a certain hour, the better it will be for your publicity. However, it all boils down to quality content, and this part of the book should explain exactly why (and most importantly, how).

Myth 1: Your Followers Care About You

As the number of followers increases, it is easy to get caught up and think that they really care about you. They like your posts after all. This illusion that just because someone hits "like" on your post, they actually like *you* can be very dangerous to some.

Imagine if you are a teenage girl posting makeup tips. The more likes and shares that she has, the more she may believe in the value of the system itself. She may even associate her own value and worth on the number of likes. Do the people who watch her videos actually care about her as a person? Unfortunately, probably not.

The truth is that most followers don't care about you or your posts. It just so happens that your post came across in their feed as they scroll catatonically through countless other posts, ads, and messages.

Although many people are using social media to promote a business or bring awareness to something, there are others who just post for the sake of posting. Do you think that their followers actually care about them? Did they stir some type of emotion in the followers?

So, if we know that your followers do not naturally care about you, the question is how do we make them care? It does sound fairly easy but consider how do we get people to actually care about us in the real world? How do you create an emotional bond with someone with whom you seemingly have nothing in common with?

Sending a Message to Your Followers

Let's start with the basics. What does it really mean for people to care about you? By definition, the word caring means to display kindness and concern for others. It is showing empathy and feelings of compassion for another person. It is touching a person in an emotional way that makes them want to or be willing to inconvenience themselves for your benefit.

We all meet random people every day. But there is no emotional bond established with each and every one of these. There is no possible way for a celebrity like Selena Gomez to have an emotional connection with each and every one of the 100+ million followers through daily, regular, generic posts.

However, if your message is able to meet a person where they are at, touching him or her through your words, pictures and actions, you will be able to create that bond and emotional connection. You have to hit them deep. Reach them in a way that they never expected. Communicate your message in such a way as to express your understanding of their hopes, fears and dreams. Allow them to use their imagination about your relationship and define it as if it is real.

If you are creating posts and messages that appeal to YOU as if you are the audience, then you probably have misread who your audience is and what they really want. Do your research. Determine who it is that you are speaking to, who you want to reach and what is it that they are hoping to receive from you. This is where the value in your message will lie. Take the extra time to research, use the vocabulary of those you are speaking to. Address the real pain points and in fact, be real!

Going back to the celebrities who have a large following. Each of them shares their real stories, and their real struggles with those who want to know. Selena Gomez for example shares her personal struggles with relationships and her career. She engages her followers and lets them know that she understands their struggles too. She shares that her success has come after trials and hardships. She is not simply posting random pictures and posts about unnecessary topics.

Let your audience project their own fantasies towards your message as well.

Learning What Makes People Tick

Great marketing is mostly about learning exactly what people care about: what makes them tick. We know that people do not really care about you when they are looking up to your service. They care about themselves, and how you may help them solve a certain problem. But in most cases, there is more to that.

People will say all kinds of nice things – but in most cases, it is all a façade. Nowadays, the average customer is well-researched, and, likely, they have already gone through countless of your competitors before they got up to you. This is why they will analyze you based on various other circumstances. The trick here is to figure out exactly what makes them tick – what they care about. Here is how you can figure that out:

- **Identify Their Problems**

When you sell a product to a client, you are not selling them a product that you just want to bring into the world: you sell a product that you believe will make their lives easier. You can't sell a customer a product unless it improves their life –

it's impractical, yet many business owners put themselves into this situation.

To find out what makes your audience tick, you need to understand who they are – and specifically, what pains they have. Your purpose here is to create a product that may alleviate that pain. Otherwise, you won't be able to get your business going.

Many small business owners are struggling to get out in the world by creating a product, and then present it to a wide audience, hoping that they can attract the right people – but in the meantime, they end up forgetting who their audience is. They are so focused on attracting potential customers that they no longer remember who they are trying to reach. They don't have their pains in mind – but a general product that might solve a certain widespread problem.

This is why, in order to connect with your audience, you need to go to the places that they currently are – no matter if it's in a physical place or a social media one. Try to talk to them regularly and learn about any problems that they might have. Look at reviews and complaints about similar products – see what their actual desires are. This way, you can create better products that you may launch at the right audience.

- **Mind the Vocabulary**

Your followers do not particularly care about you. In fact, they just care about what you say, and how your words are resonating with whatever they have in mind. They care about the way you speak, how your words connect to them.

Whenever you are speaking, not only do you have to be clear in the words that you are using, but you should also use a language that seems attractive to them. A lawyer will not attract potential customers by using the "ghetto language" – they will want to seem as professional as possible. In this case, they might want to use a few "fancy" words that will help deliver an image.

At the same time, if your audience is formed out of people such as students or stay-at-home mothers, then you might want to refrain from the extra professional language. Your fancy, pompous words will not phase them in the way that you are hoping – and in truth, it might just send them in a different direction. People are looking for the kind of language and behavior that they can connect to, not the kind that will ascertain your show-off qualities.

Bear in mind that your vocabulary should also contain "trigger words" – or as marketers refer to them, "words that sell." Certain words in your vocabulary may attract customers to your side, keeping them there with certain words that sell. They may not realize it themselves, but words such as "you," "new," or even something as simple as "tips" may earn you quite a few followers. This is because you can manage to connect to them on a deeper level – as long as you also learn how to steer clear of clichés.

The same thing goes with the vocabulary that your potential customer is using. What words are they using? Do they seem like they are trying to convey something to you? What words are they using specifically – and do they mostly consist of positive or negative words? Do they seem to be using a lot of "mhm" words or short monosyllabic responses? If that is the case, even if they are your followers or not, it is likely that you will not be able to hang on to them for very long.

By lending an ear at the words that your potential customers are using, you will be able to figure out exactly what makes them tick. What do they seem to be interested in? What exactly does it seem particularly boring to them? The richer their vocabulary, the more they might be interested in what you have to sell them. Your tone of voice will also be quite determinant, as they will be looking for someone with a calm attitude – not someone that will rush them into taking action.

- **Pay Attention to the Body Language**

When you are talking with a customer, you should pay attention to your body language and the body language of your client. Specifically, you might want to focus on the feedback that your customer is giving you – although this mostly applies to when you are speaking with the customer face to face.

Most of the advice that we receive in concerns to feedback focuses on the things that we have to say – but the non-verbal communication is very important as well. For example, by conveying discomfort or aggression using your body language, you might end up making them feel unsafe – therefore, preventing them from further listening to what you have to say. Sometimes, it's the little gestures that give away the way they feel – and all you have to do is "listen" to what their body language is telling you. If they do not feel a connection to what you are trying to convey to them through your body language, then you might just lose them in the long run.

Strategies to Influence their Behavior

When it comes down to it and you learn exactly what makes these people tick, it might be quite easy to fall inside your own trap and begin telling them exactly what they should do – but that will only work for so long. Granted, it has been proven that calls to action have been very effective in getting people to your side – but when they realize that you are only shamelessly trying to pull them over, there is a high chance that this will just backfire on you.

The best way to influence them in general and make them resonate with you is to leave just a little bit of space between your audience and your marketing message. This way, they will have all the space that they need to think about how life will be once that certain product or idea gets back. Their behavior will be influenced – and they will not even realize that it happened. You just gave them the right incentive, and they used it to create their own scenarios. Here is what you may do to draw your customers to you, but without diving too much in their personal space:

1. Engage with Them Offline and Online

We live in a digital world, where everyone is hyper-connected through every platform available on the Internet. Companies can now reach out to their clients and engage with them – but at this point, consumers have become rather skeptical with these companies, and tend to be quite suspicious when it comes to purchasing a service or product in particular.

For this reason, the best way to connect with your customers is to engage them in a conversation where they see your intentions and message as sincere. Businesses should be able to inspire their potential clients into advocating their services and products – and this is usually done if you engage them offline. You leave them that little gap where they can analyze your intentions, after which they should be able to connect with you much more efficiently.

2. Learn Your Customer's Needs

No customer likes it when you try to force your way into their personal way – but to create that space where they can make their own decisions, you need to prepare the right environment for them. For example, a lot of businesses believe that they may use social media to change or influence how their potential customers think. However, the only way in which they can do that is to create mobile-friendly pages that suit their preferences and needs. If they are not completely certain about it, they may want to create surveys that the potential customer may access – therefore, giving them the freedom to engage the platform themselves and imagine their outcome.

3. Go for the Golden Rule

There are certain benefits to being attractive, and this stretches to how websites look. A good-looking website may indirectly increase your trustworthiness and likeability – bringing potential customers closer and closer to your product. Everyone wants to look at pretty things – so it's normal to make your website look tastefully attractive to attract the crowd.

For this reason, you may use the "golden rule," "golden ratio," – or the "divine proportion," as it is sometimes referred to by various individuals. It involves picking the most visually appealing proportions, sizes, margins, column widths, line heights, and so on. The more balanced and attractive it looks, the more it should attract the customers into visiting your domain.

4. Be Available at All Times

If you wish to engage the behavior of your customer, you will have to focus on creating emotional connections with them – and this can be done through something as basic as creating

24/7 customer support. Customers crave this type of positive experience – and generally speaking, the sooner they receive a response, the happier they will be – which will definitely influence their consumer behavior.

Almost half of the customers that complain about websites or social media platforms expect to receive a response within one hour of sending the message, whereas the other half also expects messages at night and/or during weekends. This kind of availability will influence their behavior and make them connect with you – determining them choose your service or product over someone in your competition. Plus, since we pretty much live in the digital world, companies should place their focus on creating easily reachable mediums.

5. Bring the Testimonials

Every business will work particularly hard in creating a pompous, good-looking website – and the chances are very high that for some people, it will work. However, it will not work for everyone. Before making a purchase, the average consumer will first try to read as many reviews as possible to convince themselves that your product is indeed the right choice to go for.

As mentioned, it is very easy to tell people what they should do, when you are the owner of the company. However, the more you try telling people what to do, the less they will want to do it. Customers will want to convince themselves that they have made the right choice – and generally, this happens when they see that other people have tried the product and succeeded.

This is why it is always a good idea to bring testimonials into the mix. This way, you are not directly telling the customer to buy your product – but you are subtly influencing them into buying it by giving them that customer gap. You are letting them make their own decision, only influencing from the background while the client is drawing closer and closer.

In the end, it's not really that the followers and clients care about you. It's more on the lines of "they care about what you have to offer them." They care about whether this product that you are currently advertising will help them with their problem or not. They do not care about what you post on a daily basis – but they care about whether they can use those posts in their daily lives or not. In the end, you may have a subscription from your clients – but unless you manage to connect with them and attract them without actually suffocating them, it will be quite difficult for you to hang on to those subscribers.

Myth 2: More Likes and Shares are Better

We all love that feeling when you post something on Facebook or Instagram and you watch the number of LIKES go up. You feel accomplished as the volume of shares increases by the minute and you know that more and more people are viewing your message. We tend to feel better about ourselves and the message we are trying to spread as we watch the likes and shares increase.

We want the message to go viral, thinking that will increase our popularity and in turn, our money. The myth that the more likes that you have the more famous or rich you will be is simply that, a myth and will hurt your opportunities to truly be famous or rich if you let it.

In reality, likes won't pay your bills or put food on the table. The algorithms that sites like Facebook and Instagram utilize will certainly spread your message far and wide, but for what purpose. Is the number of likes truly an indicator of the success of your social media marketing?

The Marketing Measurements

As it is said, what gets measured gets done. In the case of social media marketing, what gets measured, gets the attention. The number of likes simply shows the popularity of the fan page. It does not necessarily indicate that the follower will go out and purchase the product. It displays brand awareness and knowledge. Or simply that the particular ad was attractive or appealing.

At the end of 2017, Buffer.com conducted a study of posts, which were the highest ranking for the year. A post by a photographer who had created a warped view of the world reached more than 803,000 people, was shared 2,300 times and reacted to more than 9K times. However, it did not earn any money. It was simply an engagement post. Kudos to the person who posted it for these very impressive numbers but unfortunately, it did not make this photographer a millionaire.

Another post, about Instagram marketing, received 644 reactions, reached more than 334,000 people and most importantly, was clicked on 34, 372 times. This last number is an indication that not only did viewers see the ad, but it was of interest to them and they wanted to learn more. This emotional response triggered an action. The advertiser struck a nerve, prompting more than 34K people to follow the link and engage.

This reaction, prompting an action is the key to your social media marketing. It is not the advertisement itself that will bring in the revenue, but instead the emotional response that you will incite in your potential client. That emotion, feeling or interest is what will prompt them to take action.

Consider the infamous commercials during the Half Time Show at the Super Bowl. People everywhere are at parties, the local bar or on the couch waiting with baited breath to see what the creative will put out there for your viewing pleasure. In the coffee room the next morning, the conversation typically revolves around the best and of course, worst commercials. The discussion probably swirls around the commercials even more so than the game itself. It would be an interesting study to review and evaluate the conversation surrounding both the best and worst to see which product is actually identified with each commercial. I would be willing to bet that most people could not tell you. Although they LIKED the funny commercial with the old guy, they have no idea what product it was for. The heart-wrenching ad with the kittens may have tugged at your heartstrings, but will it make you immediately go out to buy whatever it is they are selling? Probably not.

As you can see, just because someone LIKES or even shares your post or your ad, you are simply generating awareness. A person is acknowledging in a way that he/she SAW it but then quickly moves on to the next one in the news feed. Imagine scrolling down through your posts and just hitting LIKE for each and every one. Did you actually read everyone's posts? Do you understand the message that each of your friend's was trying to share? What if they asked you about it later, could you tell them what it said? Probably not. You simply acknowledged that they were active on the site and kept moving. Don't forget, there are a lot of posts to read!

The bottom line is this...is the number of likes really the best measurement of a successful post or campaign? A better way to measure is to evaluate what type of chain reaction you can begin with your posts. How many people have shared your message or talked about it with others?

Don't try to be all things to all people. Some entrepreneurs and business owners try to connect with and cater to all people. This strategy, not really a strategy at all, will diminish the value of your product and the market that you should be targeting to.

Draw a line in the sand. Figure out who in fact you should be targeting to and make a stand. Research the actual likes and dislikes of this demographic of people and focus your marketing strategy on providing them with the appropriate material to solicit an emotional response.

How will this impact you and your business you may be asking? By targeting those people with whom you can connect, you have a much better chance of them converting to an actual customer rather than simply clicking LIKE. This deceptive number or perception of popularity is still necessary but to truly gauge the value of your marketing, the number of sales that occurred as a result of your campaign is a much better measure.

Likes are the end result of a temporary feeling about your campaign. To successfully impact change and long-term sales and customers, you must focus of creating a strategy and content that will stand the test of time. In your efforts, you are looking to develop a brand that will be recognizable, memorable and longstanding.

I am sure you are familiar with many brands that have been able to endure throughout the years, amidst competition, varying promotional strategies and even challenges within the company itself. Companies like Levi Strauss, Colgate-Palmolive, Mercedes-Benz, Kraft, The New York Times and Tiffany & Co. have not only been able to endure and survive but actually come out on top.

Although times have changed and in fact, the markets may have changed, each of these companies has researched the target audience and tailored their marketing campaigns towards specific individuals with specific qualities and needs. This strategy has been used no matter whether the campaign was in print, billboard, or social media.

Just because Mercedes-Benz may have placed an amazing, historic commercial on the Super Bowl one year, and it was the topic of conversation the next day, that does not mean that the intended audience was EVERYONE who was watching at the time. The campaign was geared towards a certain type of person watching the game at the time; only that engagement will turn into a sale. It wasn't that the commercial was talked about or LIKED that made it an effective campaign. It was instead the number of people who felt a deeper connection with the message in the commercial; those who now felt that their desires, dreams and emotions were engaged and connected to are the ones who went out and in fact, purchased a Mercedes-Benz.

How will you engage your target audience?

Quality vs. Quantity – How to Make Sure You Get Quality

Some people focus a lot on the quantity of the product rather than on the quality. "The more, the merrier" – or this is how the saying generally goes. The problem is that if you wish for your marketing to be successful, you may want to focus on quality instead – because this is what matters.

In truth, both quality and quantity are important – buy you will need to create the right balance for both of them. For instance, let's say that you create a lot of posts every week, and you have quite a number of followers that like or share your product – but no one really buys it. So, while the product may seem to have potential, you haven't gone high enough to get profit.

On the other hand, if you create good quality content, it will be much easier for the followers to connect with what you have to say. Once they get engaged in your high-quality content, there is a high chance that this will also result in conversion. The more they stay on your website, the higher the chances are that they will buy something – and this can only happen if you create content that is attractive for the visitors.

The Question of "What to Measure"

So, what should you measure instead, if quantity is not something that you should put your trust in? Most people measure the likes that you get on a post – and in a way, it's good – because it gives you a good idea of how many people are interacting with your website.

But hear this: not every person that hits "like" on your post will access the link to your article/page. A lot of people will see the title, possibly agree with it, and then hit the like button as a reflex. Some may even access your post – but once they see that the quality of your post is not enough to keep them interested, they will hit "back" on that website as soon as they entered it. This will not help your website traffic much – in fact, it will only bring it down.

To make potential followers stick to your website, you need to create content that they will enjoy reading – that will give them enough reason to stay on your website for as long as it is needed to go through anything. The more they stay there, the higher the chances will be that search engines will pick on to this – deeming you as a quality website and putting you higher up the ranks.

The purpose of your post is not to get likes; everyone can get those. Nowadays, you can simply purchase those likes off the Internet – through accounts that deliver those likes to you. You can get the likes, which will make your post seem more popular – but in truth, there won't be many conversions for you there. You will need people to come in contact with your website – to get you the traffic that you deserve.

This is why instead of focusing on the likes that you get, you should focus on the traffic that your website receives. How many visitors do you get on your website on a daily basis? How much time do those people spend on your website? Do they stay there for only a few seconds, or do they spend more than a couple of minutes doing research? If they end up spending quite a lot of time there, then it's clear that your content brings them quite a lot of good information.

With each post, you are hoping to get new readers – readers that can benefit from your information. You want to help them make the right choice and inform them about the purchases that they want to make – give them all the details so that in the end, they pick you. This is why it does not make sense to focus on the likes when you need to keep them on board.

Your goal here is to measure the traffic and improve it if it's not working how you are hoping. Remember, your goal here is to get your traffic and obtain conversion – which is why you should spend less attention on the likes and more on the actual traffic.

Vanity Metrics: Why They Are a Trap

When you are just starting, it might be rather easy for you to go for any kind of metrics analysis that you can get your hands on – but sometimes, you may also want to learn how to be selective. To make an informed decision that can help you out here, you need to decide whether you want to go for actionable metrics or vanity metrics.

Actionable metrics are a key concept when it comes to this framework – and in essence, they are specific metrics that can tie repeatable and specific actions to observed results. These actionable metrics will allow you to make informed decisions for your business so that you can move closer and closer to the goal that you have in mind.

That being said, on the other end of the spectrum, we also have vanity metrics – metrics that make things look good – or at least you think they do. In truth, these metrics won't tell you if you are getting any closer to your goal or if you are just moving farther and farther away from it. Some common vanity metrics that digital marketers succumb to are:

- **CTR (Click-through-Rate):** This metric shows you exactly how many people are clicking through your website – but they do not show you the bounce rate. You may feel confident when you see the number of clicks you get every day – but if your analytics say you have an 85% bounce rate, then you can't really say that you are going anywhere with this.

- **CPC (Cost-per-Click):** Quite a high number of people go for low CPC, as they get concerned when they see a relatively high cost-per-click. However, the reason why this is a trap is that it does not really matter how much you pay for each click, as long as you get a positive investment in the returns. However, this metric works only if you manage to add the right actionable metrics as well.

- **CPA (Cost-per-Acquisition):** Just like with the CPC, the trend here is to go for the low cost per conversion. However, the metric might only show results when you already know the lifetime value of the customer – which will eventually bring a return on the investment.

Vanity metrics are quite a dangerous path to go on because they do not really show you the results in the long run. While it might not be a problem to consider them as well, they should not be used exclusively – because they will show you the metrics based on the likes and clicks rather than focusing on the bigger picture.

In the long run, you might want to try the actionable metrics – because they are the ones that will allow you to make a calculated decision. These metrics will allow you to go past the shallow clicks and move on to the ones that are relevant.

Myth 3: There Is So Much Noise, I Need to Find the Best Hack to Break Through

Noise, or things that are a distraction or not useful to you, are plentiful on social media. You are constantly hit with spam, junk email, ads for things you never knew you had searched for or even needed and even those cute little puppies. Your inbox is full of useless content and your feed is clogged with distractions.

Most people try to develop tactics to break through the noise and there are various things that have been tried. One strategy is to trick people into action. Unfortunately, this is a shortsighted strategy that focuses only on something you cannot control – those things that show up in feeds.

Instead of trying to trick people into clicking, your strategy should focus on connecting with people and bringing the discussion outside of social media. Yes. I said it. The horror! In our highly digital, technology driven world, most people cannot live a minute without their phone in their hand. They go to sleep scrolling and swiping right or left. They wake up to the alarm on their phone and before even setting foot out of the bed, they have checked email and Facebook for any new information.

The connection that you want to create to sidestep this concept of noise is to initiate a conversation online but have it continue outside of the virtual space – in the real world! You want people to be talking about it, sharing it, and yes, even dancing to it. Just like the wildly popular Gangnam Style.

Released in 2012, it became the first video on YouTube to hit 2 BILLION views. Yes, that's right! We are talking billions here! Not only were followers watching this soon to be famous video, but they were in fact sharing, liking and DOING the Gangnam style dance moves. Soon after, the artist, Psy, was accused of stealing some of his dance moves from another artist, causing controversy and of course, more discussion. Now everyone wanted to not only watch this Korean guy dance and sing, they wanted to compare it to another group's moves. The more discussion, the more traffic to the website, the more views and shares.

How does this translate to earnings? Although viewers watch videos on YouTube for free, the advertising that is displayed on the page is the revenue generator. As more and more people watched this amazing video, the more people who would see the ads, click and ultimately purchase something. According to Google's Chief Business officer, Psy's video brought in more than $8 million strictly through viewers on YouTube.

It was not a matter of how many followers Psy had or even how many people actually like him or his style. It was the conversations, the controversy and the fact that everyone needed to see what the hype was all about that drew the traffic to his video. He was able to break through the noise to create a winning product. Psy was not just another guy on the internet sharing his music. Between July and September of 2012, through word of mouth, Gangnam Style very quickly ascended the ranks of top videos and in this short time, had been viewed more than 2 million times. As the dance began to catch on, people began to record themselves dancing the Gangnam Style and posting on YouTube. This brought in additional views for Psy as viewers compared their dance to the original.

As the video began to go viral, it caught the attention of the media. Rather than Psy having to approach the media about his video to promote it and drive traffic, they were coming to HIM. The more press he received, the more traffic was driven to his video. What a truly amazing marketing campaign in which he really did not have to do much. What he did do was start a conversation in the social media landscape, which led to conversations *outside* social media. Through his music, he targeted a very specific group of people who he knew would want to listen to new, fresh music and would easily share and talk about his work.

This is how Psy broke through the noise and how you can too. It will require research and effort but, in the end, you will reap the benefits by having your products or services talked about outside of social media.

Of course, the first thing that you must do is identify your target market. Who are you selling to? What product or service will solve a problem that this particular group is interested in? Do your research and learn all that you can about this market.

Whether you start out with a following 100 or 1,000, you need to actively listen to what your audience is telling you; what do they like; what topics are regularly discussed. Utilize analytics to determine what it is they are talking about, what they react to and what posts and topics get the most attention. Listening is the first step towards writing great content that will stir a reaction in your intended audience. This emotional reaction will be the trigger for them to begin the conversation.

Through your content, you want to make your audience believe that they are important to you. Be relatable and transparent. You are not trying to trick anyone into buying or sharing information. Be your genuine self both on and offline by sharing your desire to help, influence or provide them with a benefit. When you speak to and connect with people on a level that is personal and non-salesy, you conquer the noise and develop an unbreakable bond.

In the marketing of Gangnam Style, we can only imagine what Psy's strategy was to market to his audience. His passion for music was evident in the video through his facial expressions and dance moves and he shared his love with his audience. This came through as a feel-good reaction which viewers just felt compelled to share with others. He connected with his audience on a deeper level than simply a new, upbeat song. He caused that emotional reaction that you should also be trying to obtain from you viewers, willing them to share it with others.

By getting to know your target audience, you can create great content about things that are important to them and about things that will help them create a better life. Pictures also speak a thousand words. When considering what will touch a person emotionally and will spark that further discussion, consider what visually sparks your interest. What pictures on Instagram make you pause your scrolling to look more carefully at it? What images take your breath away and then encourage you to show it to a friend or family member? Maybe it stirs an emotion that prompts a discussion.

This same emotion that is stirred within you is what you want to bring out for your followers. You want to use photos that will not only speak a thousand words to them but that they will in turn, speak a thousand words about. Your audience is the best promotion that you could ask for when the conversation is taken out of social media and into the real world. Inevitably, those that they talk about it with will come back to social media to see it for themselves or to join the online conversation.

Through your outstanding message and content, you can take a small group of diligent and faithful followers and turn them into your marketing army. By consistently sharing the same message, you establish yourself as reliable, trustworthy and knowledgeable. People will see you as someone who cares about their needs which will in turn, build your reputation and encourage them to discuss and share.

Consider the local motivational speaker who regularly posts inspirational and motivational content. He knows what it is that his followers want and what they react to. His content continuously creates an emotional response within each and every person that it touches. His message is shared countless numbers of times on social media and discussed between friends. New followers seek out his websites to hear his inspiring words for themselves. His message is no longer simply another of the many inspiring messages that pass through the news feed, adding to the social media noise. They have instead become sought after, daily nuggets of affirmation. Each and every follower feels the connection with the speaker as if they are personal friends, and the valuable feelings that go with it.

Myth 4: Post X Times Per Day at Exactly X O'clock

I have to post every day at the same time to ensure that my audience is available and ready to receive my message. NOT!

When it comes to social media marketing, we tend to focus on how many times per day and what time we post. This strategy assumes that people only check their social media feeds at certain times and does not take into account the other more important factors.

If you have done your research, you will already understand that when people are interested in a particular topic, they will follow and view your content. By connecting with your small group of followers, your targeted audience, you can be assured that they will see it. They want to see it and if you are being consistent, with powerful and fulfilling content, they will seek it out no matter what time of day or what day of the week you post it.

Studies of trends in social media originally suggested that to reach the maximum number of followers and to increase your engagement, you had to post during commuting time, lunch and break times, and evenings. This slightly outdated information has not been updated with new trends and to cover unique target groups.

Rather than focusing on the specific times and days that you should be posting, instead focus on what works best for YOUR followers. By having an understanding of the habits and social media routines of your audience, you can better determine what will be the best time to post to gain the most exposure for your content.

The key here is for YOUR content. Each target market or audience will have its own best time to post. For example, if you are targeting moms of young children, you can be pretty sure that rush hour and mid-afternoon will NOT be appropriate times to post content. They will be too busy getting kids on and off the bus or to and from school to notice your post. However, if you post at 9pm, you might be more likely to get their attention after the children are settled in for the night and finally get some "me" time to scroll through social media. It may even be their guilty pleasure for the day, the only time they have to read something that interests them. Because this may be a similar time for others as well, they may not only see it, but share it and then chat about it at tomorrow's PTA meeting since it will be fresh in their minds.

On the other hand, if you are promoting a new deli that has just opened up in town, you may want to post and share mouth-watering pictures of the delicacies that you offer at 11am each day. You can be pretty sure that people will be searching for lunch options around this time and what better time to engage not only their senses but their stomachs as well. If they then come in to purchase lunch from your deli, you can now establish a deeper connection in person, encouraging them to start a conversation off of social media as well with others to stop in and enjoy your food.

When it comes to social media, of course, your goal should be to gain the most engagement within the first few hours of posting. Studies have shown that the likelihood of your post being seen decreases as the time goes on. Going back to the deli, it would not be a good idea to post about your new lunch specials AFTER the lunch rush. At that point, you would simply be adding to the social media noise as your followers scroll past your post on their way to find something else that interests them.

Have you ever heard your friend say "did you see Jane's post last week?" Unless you saw it shortly after Jane posted it, it is highly possible that the noise in your social media feed has overpowered Jane's post and it is no longer visible or even relevant any longer. That being said, you need to capitalize on the momentum of engagement and not only post but engage with your audience while they are available.

If you recall, earlier in this book we discussed proactively connecting with and reactively connecting with your audience. By interacting with them during this time after you post, you are reinforcing your concern for them and their importance to you. As you receive comments on your posts, be sure to respond as soon as possible.

However, we have also seen that trends have changed as many people pick up their phones to mindlessly scroll through their social media feeds before they even set foot out of bed. So, in reality, no matter what time of day, or how many times you post, either your followers will see it or they won't. There is no perfect time or pre-determined number of times per week that contains the magic number to guarantee that followers will see it and engage.

Instead, focus on producing great content and posting regularly, whatever that means to you. Maybe it is once per day or once per week, but create a regular schedule of posting so that your followers will look forward to receiving your engaging content at that particular time. By consistently posting amazing content, you will automatically draw people in as loyal followers who are willing to share and discuss with their friends.

Another problem with social media posting is the actual algorithms that are behind the scenes running the show. Have you ever wondered how it is that they know that you recently searched for a place to take a new yoga class? The algorithms and science behind social media pick up on your trends, your searches and views and will automatically send you posts and advertisements that coincide with these. It is as if Big Brother is truly watching – hello *1984*! George Orwell's prophetic book, written in 1948, describes a society in the future in, which all citizens are watched. It does make you feel like someone is watching when suddenly you see these ads for something that you were recently looking for pop up on your screen. But this is how the algorithm's work and they change. However, you cannot plan your post timing based on these or any assumptions that your content will automatically get shared to someone who was searching for it.

Finding your exact social media sweet spot is overrated. There is no such thing as the perfect time to post or the magic formula for the right combination of when and how many times to post. People check their social media posts all of the time so they will at some point see your posts. The key to success stems from focusing your content and posts on what is important for your audience, tailoring your message to truly what will impact your followers and spark that emotional response. So, no matter what time you choose to post, make sure your message is consistent, relevant and emotionally charged. The sweet spot will lie there right in your hands.

Myth 5: My Product Doesn't Sell – Fix It with More Ads

My product isn't selling, it must be that I am not advertising it enough. I will fix it by placing more ads online. Really? Just because Facebook is telling you that you should Boost your post, doesn't mean that is the best way to go. It is no guarantee though that just because you spend the money to advertise that you will in fact reap any return on your investment at all.

It is very common for business owners, especially new entrepreneurs, to consider social media ad campaigns as the cure-all solution for selling a product or building a following. Many people believe that as long as we spend money on advertising, everything will work out just fine. I am not saying that paid advertising is not necessarily required. What I am saying is that it will not solve all of your problems or drive traffic to your website. It is by far a quick fix!

Let's look at a small non-profit organization looking to drive traffic to their website with the hope that people will see value in the services offered, the lives they impact and they will be moved to donate to the cause. The organization has a $1000 budget for the year for advertising expenses and they believe that their $1000 should convert to possibly thousands of dollars in donation revenue. Unfortunately for them, even with their good intentions, the ads have not driven the traffic to their website nor earned them any significant money in donations.

On its own, the non-profit's website does not convert followers to philanthropists so executives sought for a magic solution to their problem, thinking that social media ads were going to be their golden egg. Sadly, after spending too much money on ads, the organization received no donations at all.

Then there are of course those companies who do virtually no advertising, yet seem to come out on top. The fashion retailer, Zara, carefully studies their customers' desires and listens to what they want. Information is sent back to the design team daily, sharing what it is customers are looking for. This ingenious way of design development and producing what it is the customers want has inspired customers to share through word of mouth this incredible process. No advertising required!

Companies whose main objective is to meet a need will find that very little advertising is required. Each of the following companies followed several similar tactics in their marketing strategy instead of advertising and as you will see, they all have come out on top:

Costco, the second largest retailer in the world, does not do any advertising. By getting to know their customers first, they were able to achieve their success by customers sharing their amazing experiences in the store by word of mouth.

With products geared towards the adrenaline-junkie, GoPro established its presence in the market through its online videos, which depict other adventure seekers in action. The founders researched their target market and just knew that those who are on the constant search for the adrenaline rush would not be able to resist sharing the amazing stunts and feats that their fellow junkies had recorded. Thrill-seekers around the world shared information about the videos and camera products, building a community of others videotaping their own outdoor adventures. No advertising needed!

The award winning product produced by Tesla requires no fancy ads for you to know what it is. Executives at Tesla rely on the quality of their electric vehicle and the surge in environmental concern to propel the company's sales without spending a dollar on advertising. See for yourself how people talk after one of these high-tech, sleek vehicles passes them on the highway.

Word spreads like wildfire when someone has experienced excellent service, found a great product or feels important and respected. On the other hand, word of mouth can work against you as well. Have you ever had a poor experience at a restaurant and very quickly posted a negative review about your experience? People searching for a new restaurant read these reviews and they can weigh very heavily on someone's choice to dine there or not. As much as word of mouth is a good thing, it can also work against you if you have not ensured you meet all of the customers' requirements and needs.

The online retailer, Zappos, was built with word-of-mouth as their only marketing strategy. Spending their advertising budget instead on customer service, they have become one of the largest online retailers of clothing and shoes. Their strategy of excellent customer service has driven repeat business while word-of-mouth has continued to bring in new customers to experience it as well.

For each of these companies, there was, in fact, a formula to their success, which you can apply to your products and services as well. We will discuss in more detail in the next chapter how to use social media properly to help you attain the results you are looking for.

Five Questions to Ask Yourself If Your Ads Aren't Working

No matter if you are a beginner in the business or if you have already been going at it for some time, there is a chance that you might stumble over this issue: your ads are not working anymore. You might get all the clicks and likes – but the conversion isn't there. Countless people are clicking on your ads, and on the surface, everything seems successful. You're getting the likes and the clicks, so why does it seem like you aren't getting anywhere with them?

The average person tries to fix this problem by adding more ads – but does this really help? If your ad wasn't working in the first place, should your solution be to create even more ads? All of them might lead to the same result. Think about it: if your ads aren't successful, you cannot expect that everything will be different if you add more of the same thing – you need to make a few modifications first.

As mentioned, clicks and likes don't do much unless the visitor has an interest in what you are trying to sell. You may be an expert in using a program such as AdWords, but if the problem lies beneath the ad, then you might want to work on the underlying cause rather than on the symptoms. Social media ads are no longer the way they used to be in the past – so, if you noticed that things are going slightly (or heavily) downward, you might want to begin troubleshooting. Here are a few questions that you may want to ask yourself if your ads are not working for you.

1. Am I targeting the wrong people?

One of the main reasons why social marketing seems to fail is because business owners don't target their ads properly. Facebook allows you to create a target audience – but very few people manage to notice this.

Think about it: there are about 1.09 billion people that are currently on Facebook. Kids are using it, parents are using it – your grandmother is probably using it too. There are quite a lot of people in the world using it, so you can't say that your target audience is not on the platform. They're there; they just can't see your ad. This applies for pretty much every ad on every social media platform ever.

No matter if you are using Facebook ads or any other kind of social media ads, the main perk here is that you may get to target those ads so that they may appear to a very precise audience – one that will show interest in your product. These people will click on those ads out of curiosity (because they have been looking for that product) – which may in return lead to a conversion for you. This feature is exactly why there has been a growth in advertisements over the past few years.

However, the downside is that if you target your ads poorly, you may not get any conversion. Let's say that you made a very beautiful ad that shows you sell merchandise for rock festivals, but instead of reaching the people that are interested in it, it's going to people who enjoy going to pop concerts, for example. Both are good genres, but unless the people have an actual interest in them, it will not lead to conversion on your end.

The same thing applies if you are selling handmade snowshoes (just an example) in Canada. If the people seeing your ad are in Florida or Australia, it's obvious that you probably will not get any conversions. They might not need those items, and they might not want to spend all that time and money on the shipping. Or maybe you don't even have a pet, but ads keep trying to sell dog food to you – no matter how awesome that ad looks like, you won't need to buy that product.

The examples here are endless. This is exactly why you need to think about the people that you are targeting. If you are targeting the wrong people, you will be getting quite a lot of bounce – from individuals that may be just curious but have no actual intention of buying. Those "curiosity clicks" will not only cost you money, but they will also lead to poor conversion.

In order to efficiently target your ads, you may want to first take a good look at your clients and try to build a profile of the ideal customer. By knowing the characteristics and traits of the customer that you believe is the ideal one, you should be able to set up those ads so that they only appear to the right people.

Here, you might want to take the time to create a "buyer persona" – someone that is most likely to buy the product from you. Here is the information that you will usually have to keep in mind:

- Location

- Gender

- Age

- Who or what influences them

- Hobbies and interests

- Language

The world of ad creation might seem rather confusing – but at the same time, it is intuitive. You may go for the option of everyone seeing your ads – but the more you target them, the better your conversion should be.

2. Is my offer that bad? Am I not bidding correctly?

One more reason why Facebook ads might not be working for you is that you are not making the correct bids. Your offers are simply not attractive to your target customers and aren't generating any clicks – in which case you might want to make some slight adjustments to the bidding section.

Most people go for the automatic bid, as it allows the social media platform to set the bids so that you get the most clicks and likes at a good price – but if that fails, you may want to manually set a bid amount. With that, you should be able to set how much you are willing to bid, depending on how much you can afford. At that point, you will be able to see a suggested amount for the bid per click.

This concerns you, as the seller – but when it comes to finances, you will have to consider the viewer. If your offer is too expensive, it might have nothing to do with the ad itself – but with the prices set behind that ad. If your viewers perceive what you have to sell as being "too expensive," it's obvious that they will not even give your ads the time of day. In this case, you will have to fix your offer to make it more attractive to the customer.

Here, you might want to go for the help of a market strategist. They will analyze exactly how much your competition sells their products with, how you should fix your prices in accordance with that and give them the benefit of a better offer.

Once the customers see an offer that they are interested in, one that won't drill a hole through their budgets, they will certainly start clicking those ads and improve your traffic.

3. Why are people clicking my ads but aren't following through?

Many business owners tend to be confused when it comes to viewing their ad clicks. They see that they get a lot of clicks, which gives them a false sense of accomplishment. "People are clicking through my ads, so my business must have success, right?" Well, not exactly. Your business may have a lot of clicks through ads – but if no one buys what you have to offer, it's like creating a free exposition with no art sold at the end of the day. In the end, you pay for the rental, the work – and you don't even get your money's worth back.

So, why aren't people creating conversion for your posts? This may be because of a variety of reasons – however, in most cases, it might be because your post is lacking the necessary text to keep your viewers interested. Indeed, the aspect of the ad creates a very strong initial impact. Still, there are other things that you might want to keep in mind – and that is exactly what your viewers will see once they click onto your ad.

Let's say that you have a very good picture on an ad – one that gets quite a lot of people curious. So, these people will click through your ads, generating a bit of traffic – but once they get to the website itself, things change.

When viewers click onto an attractive ad, they expect to see a website that is just as catchy – which is why so many ads get quite a lot of bounce. Imagine that instead of a website nicely following the golden rule, you have one that follows no rule – and looks exactly like someone allowed a kindergartner to play with crayons there.

Many times, people focus mostly on the ads rather than on the text and SEO itself. The text ends up being badly written, it lacks proper grammar – and overall, it is all just very confusing. When they see exactly what is happening to the text that you are trying to advertise, they will lose the trust they have in you as a company. You wouldn't trust a "professional" that would not be able to spell out two words, would you?

This is why, aside from the image on the ad, you may also want to focus on the content that is on the actual website. Sure, the ads will get them on the website – but what will keep them there is the content that you make available for the readers.

Users might also not be interested in creating more conversion because you are not exactly truthful in the ads about what you have to offer. Countless companies are creating fancy and beautiful ads with a variety of products or services that they have to sell – but when those interested users click onto the ad, they see that what you are offering is slightly different from what you were talking about in the ad. It might be about different products – or it might concern different prices. What is clear is that the failure of sticking to what you are advertising is exactly what is keeping the customers from coming.

4. Are my ads not click-worthy?

Let's say that you have great content, a decent offer, and you are also targeting the right audience – but you still don't seem to get the audience that you need. Your ads aren't getting enough clicks, and your product or service does not seem to be getting exposure – not to mention the fact that you are not getting any conversion for your service.

If you already made certain to respect all of those mentions above, then it might be a sign that the thing you need to fix is how your ad looks. In most cases, you are generally able to tell how your ad's creativity is performing by looking at whether it has a low CTR or not.

Facebook CTRs, for instance, have an average of 0.9% - but the percentage will be different depending on the type of ad that you are running. For example, if you have a right sidebar ad, you will want to be around a 1% CTR, whereas a newsfeed ad should ideally be above 5%.

Social media platforms such as Facebook or Instagram are also seen as visual platforms. Therefore, if you want to attract people to your page, you should make sure that your ads are as eye-catching as possible. We live in an era where people keep sharing the visually-appealing stuff – so, your job here is to give them what they want.

5. Am I not using enough calls to action?

You may either not have any call-to-action stacked upon your text, or it may just be mudded or missing the point. Regardless, it might be one of the big reasons why your ads are falling short. Since ads do not have a lot of space underneath (particularly when it comes to sidebar ads), people tend to skip the call-to-action. They are hoping that the image and offer itself will be attractive enough to trigger them into action.

However, in order to catch the users' interest (along with their clicks), you may want to have a concise call-to-action set on your ad. This way, you will tell them what you wish for them to do – and this will work on a subconscious level. Plus, aside from your ad, you may also want to add calls to action on your landing page, as it will further improve conversion.

A good way to ensure that your call to action goes across is to put it directly on your ad. You may choose from options such as "Learn more" or "Shop now" – small words that are just enough to trigger people into action. Not only do calls to action improve your click-through rate, but they are also more likely to help you improve your purchase rate.

Part II: How to Use Social Media

For years, it has been proven that social media is quite an efficient way to get some new leads – as long as you know precisely how to use it to your advantage. Social media can connect you with quite a lot of people, bring you a fair audience – and overall, make you extremely popular in the long run. By putting your product online and advertising it on social media, you may just end up increasing your revenue – particularly if that platform is very popular among the people.

Social media has become quite popular also because you can post advertisements. Facebook, for example, allows you to post ads and share your posts at all times – all while increasing the visibility to the audience that you are currently attempting to target. The more people share your posts, the higher the chances are that your product will become more and more popular.

Social media can get you quite a lot of leads if you know exactly what tools to use. You need to know what to post, where to post – and also how to post. As long as you are familiar with how a particular platform works, you should be able to use it to your advantage so that more and more people get acquainted with your product – which should result in you getting as much conversion (a.k.a. purchases) as you want.

That being said, care should also be exercised in this regard. Social media is quite a convenient tool – but unless you take the necessary precautions, you might just end up causing more damage than good to your business. Before you know it, you will be losing all your leads – and that is the last thing that you want to happen.

The best way to ensure that not everything is lost in the blink of an eye is to be smart about your strategy. While you should have a main platform where you conduct your business, you should not leave it all there. You may want to use other platforms as well – and the reason for that is a story that we will dive into later on.

Social media can be a very efficient tool to increase the number of followers for your business, but you just need to understand it. You must know which platform has a higher rate of success, which one to be particularly careful about – and what you have to do to "spread out" your business as much as possible. A good businessman or businesswoman will make use of all the tools made readily available for them.

The Use of Different Marketing Platforms

Let us be completely honest: in this day and age, if anyone ever thinks about going into business, there is one big platform that they will use – Facebook. With the billions of users that are currently on that platform, it feels like the smartest decision, doesn't it? You can target your ads, and you may attract relevant customers to your niche – earning you not only good conversion but also faithful customers.

And if you think about it, the idea is quite sound. Think about the number of likes that your product can get – and it is more likely that people will see you in a Facebook ad rather than in a Google search. With today's use of social media, most people log onto Facebook every few minutes, scroll for a bit, laugh at a few memes – and in the meantime, see a few ads. You don't see them going on Google for these things. So, it would make sense why a campaign on Facebook would be the most appropriate action.

However, here's a thought: what if, one day, Facebook would cease to exist? Let's say that one day, Mark Zuckerberg decided that he no longer wanted to go with Facebook – that he wanted to create a platform that is more popular and more efficient. What if Facebook would slowly go into the background and become a distant memory?

Before you go and say that "that's not possible!" think about MySpace. Think about how popular it used to be before Facebook appeared. At that point, every cool kid and every big business had a MySpace account – and aside from the people that did not know how to use a computer, everyone was connected on MySpace. A few years ago, if you wanted to become successful, you had to start with MySpace.

And there was a business at some point that did exactly that: they conducted all of their marketing moves on MySpace and became quite popular. People were opting for their services, sharing their content – they were pretty much everywhere on the ads of MySpace. And that was exactly the problem: they were *only* on MySpace, and no other platforms.

You can imagine that this was rather problematic when MySpace fell through and the platform failed. A platform that was once so successful suddenly started losing all of its people – all of them migrating to Facebook, Instagram, and all the other "cool websites." The company in question lost all of its followers, practically overnight – and they could never recover from the loss. This was simply because they no longer had the clients following them since they put all their faith in MySpace and refused to go with other social media platforms as well.

This is why it is recommended that you post content on other marketing channels as well. Go for the ones that seem most reliable to last throughout the years. For example, let's say that Facebook is a good idea to adopt for some quality marketing right now – but aside from that, you should also pick platforms that have been there for quite some time. The email, for example, has been here for more than 50 years – so, investing in a good email campaign is not a bad idea.

This is because even nowadays, email marketing is the number one communication channel. Most consumers tend to check their email on a daily basis, and there is a much higher chance of your visibility increasing by using this platform.

Plus, unlike Facebook that filters who sees your content (only a small number of people that liked your page will see your content on their newsfeed), email marketing will let everything go through. You control who sees the subject of your content. Once it goes into the inbox, it is all a matter of whether your follower is interested in the title or not. In this regard, you should focus on creating catchy headlines that will increase your open rate – all while focusing on great content.

Social media offers you quite a low visibility, which is why you shouldn't put all your followers there. You can decrease that vulnerability by also touching up on your email marketing strategy.

Platforms for Reliable Social Media Marketing

We have touched upon the fact that for a business to be successful, you might want to start marketing it on more than one platform. Some platforms are more efficient than others – with greater possibilities and a higher "people pool" – but in order for your campaign to be profitable, you may want to try marketing it on at least two of the following platforms:

1. Facebook

Facebook is likely one of the most popular ways to do your marketing right now, mostly thanks to the Facebook ads and the people galore that are currently scrolling through the website. Plus, Facebook is continuously updating, creating reliable ways for you to reach your audience and make your products all the more popular.

One great way to do modern marketing is to use the Facebook Live option – an amazing method to engage people in video offers. Bear in mind that this feature needs quite a bit of strategizing, as it involves reaching out to the audience in a moment when they can actually answer your lives. For instance, it might be more efficient to do those lives in the evening, or early in the morning, when people are not caught up with work, school or classes. If they are busy, it is obvious that you will not be able to reach them in the middle of the day.

That being said, the sponsored ads on Facebook are also a great way of making yourself known. It is a platform that has the potential of sustaining an actionable audience – making it a good choice for small business owners and big corporations alike.

2. Instagram

One big reason why this platform is so popular is that it is very easy to use. All you have to do is snap a picture and make a post. It is a good social media platform for those whose businesses are focused more on visual aesthetics rather than technical details.

The only disadvantage here is that since it is a "visual platform" that focuses mostly on pictures and hashtags, you can't really do a lot in the area of text content creation. The content is rather ephemeral – so, unless you make some aesthetically appealing posts that can generate clicks, there is a very good chance that your content will go all the way down to the bottom.

3. LinkedIn

LinkedIn is also quite an efficient way to get your business going, mostly because that's the platform everyone goes to for "official business." It's the platform where everyone goes looking for a job, to advertise their product – or to look for a certain company in a particular industry.

It is not like Facebook, for example, where people are going there for every purpose (e.g. social connection, entertainment, etc.). People go on LinkedIn because they are actually looking for something – which is why you should consider using this platform.

4. Twitter

Twitter might seem like an easy platform to use – but the truth is relatively far from that. Even though all you have to do is post something in 140 characters (with spaces), it might be rather difficult to deliver something meaningful in such a small word count.

By itself, Twitter has the ability to create quite a large audience very quickly, and only attracts those that are interested in your domain. Indeed, it is still impossible at this point to directly message your followers (which might make you feel like you are throwing everything in the wind), but it's not a deal-breaker. In fact, the platform is a great way for you to connect with various followers, sending them to your other platforms (such as a blog or a podcast).

How to Do Basic Email Marketing

Email marketing is quite an efficient way to increase the visibility of your brand – mostly because you know for certain that the email will end up in the inbox of your subscriber. However, to gain profit, you need to ensure that those emails lead to good open rates conversion.

It is not that difficult to perfect your email marketing skills –
you just need to know exactly what steps to follow.

1. Use Opt-In Offers

When people see a random ad of a product on your page, they
might not be as inclined to give you their email. However, if
you use the right "bait," – in other words, an opt-in – people
will have more reasons to subscribe. To get people to leave
you their email, give them something they can't say no to –
like a freebie or a discount. They'll be more eager to connect
if you give them a taste of your product.

2. Send Emails Regularly

A good way to build trust with your customers is to send
emails regularly – and also think carefully about the emails
that you are planning to send. You might want to send emails
where you are promoting your products – but as stated
above, you also need to listen to your audience and connect
with them. Emails containing surveys or questions will allow
you to get the feedback that you need so that you may
improve your strategy over time.

3. Segment Your List

The service you have might provide a variety of features and
have different followers. New followers, old followers,
inactive followers, or followers that have a particular
interest; you need to learn their behavior and preferences so
that you can only send them what they need. This is why you
might want to segment your list so that each category of
followers gets the content they are interested in.

4. Create the Right Content

You might have a catchy opt-in and good timing – but if your content is not good enough, then it will not lead to conversion. The good news about email is that you are free to create a longer email – the type that tends to feel more honest and open. It is the advantage that email has over social media – but you also need to learn how to connect with the person behind the screen rather than the prospective buyer. This way, your email marketing strategy should pay off.

Things to Do on Social Media to Get Leads

When you are trying to get your product out there, there are several things that you might want to do in order to get lead. The more efficient you are at it, the better it will be for your leads – so, here is what you may want to do:

- **Post in Groups**

No matter if you are doing your marketing on Facebook, LinkedIn or any other platform, then you may want to take advantage of the group section. These groups are found in quite a variety of subject areas, which means you are bound to find professionals in the topic – as well as people that are interested in it.

That being said, instead of making all your posts on your page itself, you may want to post in groups as well. These groups will bring you to your target audience much faster, mainly because they will have already gathered in one place. For example, if your service involves cat food, a good group to post in would be one for cat lovers.

Bear in mind that even if it's possible to join as much as 50 groups, you may want to place your efforts on just a few of the right ones. Browse the inventories for a good group match, join the relevant discussions and conversations, and consistently post your content on that topic.

- **Host Competitions and Giveaways**

If you have been using Facebook or Instagram, you may have noticed that there are quite a few brands and pages that offer giveaways. "Share this post, tag a friend, and earn a chance to win something," is what most of these posts tend to say. These giveaways are not because the brands are oh-so-generous – it's because it's a good tactic to raise awareness for your brand and grow your following.

Think about it: the more people like, comment, and tag your content, the higher the chances are that your visibility on social media will increase. Facebook and Instagram algorithms, for example, are quite smart in this area and can recognize the growing interest in your product – earning you even more exposure. A nicely made contest will not only generate brand awareness and grow your following, but it will also increase your email list and jumpstart your engagement.

- **Pay for Ads**

Running ads on social media may fulfill a variety of goals – one of them is actually generating leads from the right audience. If you go for promoted Facebook ads, for example (which is an engaging form of Facebook advertising), you are practically highlighting your posts in the newsfeed of those people.

Indeed, Facebook is not in the slightest conductive to the main sales. However, you may build trust with the users by consistently posting on that topic and engaging in communication with them. If set correctly, these sponsored ads should only appear to the right group of people, giving you the leads that you require.

What to Post on Social Media?

There are hundreds of things that you may post on social media, all of which are directly related to your business. You just need to decide which one works best at this point for your business. By making the right choice, you should be able to increase your brand awareness. Here are just a few of the countless ideas that you may post on social media – and that are very likely to get you leads.

1. Industry Articles

Not every person that has liked your page or used your product knows everything about your domain – which is why you need to deliver that information to them. This will keep him or her loyal to you because you are sharing content of informative or educational value for them.

Bear in mind that these articles should by no means be random. If you want to generate leads, you may want to learn some basic copywriting skills and improve your SEO (we'll learn later on how to do that as well). By posting well-written content related to your industry on social media, you should be able to generate leads and become the best in your field.

2. Before and After Pictures

Let's say that you are selling a product that would lead to a great transformation. It may be a new hair dye, a face mask, a weight loss program, or even cabinet paint – whatever leads to a significant change. To prove its effectiveness and to get your leads, you may want to post before and after pictures that will showcase the effect of that product.

The transformation that you are showing may be personal, or it may be related to your business. For example, you may show before and after pictures of your website redesign. Or if you are a nutritionist, you may post before and after pictures of your customer's refrigerator – post-cleaning it. These small things are surely going to get potential customers interested.

3. Behind the Scenes Videos

Followers are curious by nature – which is why a good thing to do would be to post behind the scenes videos. Share a few pictures of what's happening when you are working (try to catch the moments when you are going your hardest at it), and get your followers interested. Something good to post would be the location of a project, your office, or a special event that your company is hosting. This will allow customers to connect with you on a personal level.

4. How-to Posts

How-to posts are also quite popular among followers. Here, you may share a blog post or a video showcasing how to do something specific – but that would also appeal to the ideal customer. Obviously, it should also appeal to your niche.

Let's say, for example, that your business is related to the wedding industry. In this case, you might want to make a post or a video on how to create decorations on a budget – or a photo booth for your wedding reception. You may opt for the help of other people that are skilled in the post creation – but if you use someone else's video, you might want to tag the creator of the video as well. This technique known as back linking might not only help them, but it might also bring clients from their page to yours.

5. Tips Articles

Time-saving tips, money-saving tips, quick hacks – these types of posts are quite popular among followers. For example, if you post promotional content about what you are selling, there is a chance that the followers will not click because they are not interested at that point. However, once they see post-market "tips," there's a part of their brain that will "activate" and make them curious.

You might think that giving them tips will not exactly help your product – but somewhere in the back of their minds, your followers will be influenced. For example, let's say that you are selling homemade cleaning solutions. In this case, an article on "tips to clean your house" might seem like it's just giving them general tips – but in truth, it will just make them more interested in cleaning products. This way, you are indirectly influencing them to buy your product.

What If I Don't Get Leads?

If you aren't getting any leads, then it means that the tactic you are currently using is not effective. The campaign you are using might be poorly strategized, the budget might be wrong, or the campaign objective was not very well-thought-of. If you see that you aren't getting any leads, then you might want to ask yourself the following questions:

- **Am I giving value to my customers?**

You might think that you are selling an amazing product that can change the lives of your customers – but it might only be changing *your* life and be of no value to others. Think of the ideal customer, create a profile for them – and try to determine exactly who in your area might benefit from this product. You might want to create surveys to learn what the clients want and how to provide them valuable products.

- **Am I timing things properly?**

Let's say that you are launching a new product, and you are offering people a free trial for it. Many companies will only ask at the end of the trial, or when the client has subscribed to the full product – but the best time to reach them is *before* that trial comes to an end. Halfway through the trial, for example, you might want to ask the followers what their experience was with your product. If you see complaints, try to fix them. This way, you will be getting more leads as there will be more clients to buy the full product.

- **Am I using the right metrics?**

If you aren't getting any leads, the chances are that your current event metrics are not exactly reliable. They may be focused more on the quantity of the contacts that came onto your page rather than on the quality (i.e. vanity metrics), and they are not telling you how many of those contacts are "bouncing." If the metrics are the problem, try shifting your focus on the ones that are based on the quality.

- **Am I posting the right content?**

Sometimes, the reason for you not getting any leads might be as simple as "your content is not interesting enough." It may be because you are not posting content to the interest of your customers (content that might bring them informational value), or it might be that your content is simply boring, confusing, or badly written. In this case, if the customer is not content with what you are posting, then it is quite clear that you won't be generating any leads.

If this happens, there are two ways for you to go: first, you might want to try honing your copywriting skills. Learn a few tips and tricks, and if you already have a way with words, then this should be easy for you – with a little bit of practice. On the other hand, if you do not have the skills, then you might want to hire someone that has the necessary knowledge to give you this advantage.

In most cases, just a few changes in your marketing campaign should be enough to get you the leads that you need. Just figure out what went wrong, and try to correct each pressing matter.

Developing Copywriting Skills for Social Media Marketing

For your marketing campaign to be successful, you need to work on your SEO – and in most cases, this involves putting your copywriting skills to the test. Granted, when you own a big corporation, you can hire your own marketing department and they will take care of everything – but if your business is just starting and you see that you aren't getting much in terms of leads, then you should fix the problem. And in this regard, you might want to try honing your own copywriting skills. Here is how you may develop your skills to create good copy.

- **Write Amazing Headlines**

The headline is likely the first thing you see when it comes to content marketing. Think about it: whenever someone clicks on a link, it's because the title catches their interest – so if the title is vague or seems boring, it is likely that your followers will simply scroll through your posts and not give them even one-second thought. Make them unique and catchy and try to grab their interest – but without giving away the conclusion of the article. People are always making fun of click baits, but they are indeed effective (as long as they are relevant for the article) – particularly if you mix them with high-quality content on the landing page.

- **Imitate the Writers that You Admire**

There is a very big difference between imitating and plagiarizing. Stealing someone else's work and claiming it as your own is a big no-no. However, there's honor in using it as inspiration. For example, if your favorite writer uses humor in their texts, use that too. On the other hand, if they use more serious texts and seem to be benefiting from it, you might want to try using that as well. Use them as your source of inspiration and create some quality texts.

- **Keep It Brief and Interesting**

People will not go through paragraphs that take up half a page, regardless of how spectacular that content will be. On average, if they see that the article goes down countless pages and with paragraphs that are longer than 10 lines, they will hit "back" before you can even prove your text quality.

This is exactly why you should make it sound simple and sweet, all written in short paragraphs. This way, people will be able to skim through your content and find the information that they need. The secret to being a good copywriter is to give them the content that they need, without beating around the bush.

Conclusion

Social media is an amazing, powerful tool that can transform your business into a successful, well-oiled machine if you use it strategically to your advantage. It is my hope that through this book, I have provided you with information and things that you should avoid doing as well as those that you should do in order to succeed.

Keep in mind that your goal is to ultimately increase your sales revenue organically by providing compelling content, connecting with people and establishing a relationship. Instead of hunting for likes, tricking into clicking methods or building a massive social media following, you want to create these relationships through your ability to provide them with what they need, to express it in a way that each person feels heard and feels an emotional connection, and in turn spreads your message to others by word of mouth.

Start by avoiding the myths and continue by building a clear strategy to make your brand more popular. Don't focus on the clicks – but instead, see what those clicks result in. Use the tools, skills, and strategies that you have on hand to make your email list grow while focusing on the right clients. Because after all, you may have a lot of people subscribed to your page – but unless they actually do something (i.e. buy your service or product), it is all for nothing.

What to read next

It's a lot easier to market an excellent product that you know your audience wants then trying to convince them to buy something they don't want.

In our book *Three Key Marketing Strategies*, we tell the story of how the social platform Burbn struggled to gain traction. The founders of Burbn thought long and hard of what do to before they re-launched as Instagram.

If you don't want to buy that book now, but you're interested in getting up to date marketing tactics and strategies every month right to your inbox, consider signing up to our monthly marketing email.

Visit our site at sunbirdmarketing.com